THE GHOSTLY TALES OF

VIRGINIA'S BLUE RIDGE HIGHLANDS

For Megan

Published by Arcadia Children's Books
A Division of Arcadia Publishing
Charleston, SC
www.arcadiapublishing.com

Spooky America is a trademark of Arcadia Publishing, Inc.

First published 2021

Manufactured in the United States

ISBN: 978-1-4671-9828-8

Library of Congress Control Number: 2021938379

Notice: The information in this book is true and complete to the best of our knowledge. It is offered without guarantee on the part of the author or Arcadia Publishing. The author and Arcadia Publishing disclaim all liability in connection with the use of this book.

Images courtesy of Shutterstock.com; pp. 8, 28, 50, 58, 80, 96 courtesy of Joe Tennis.

Spooky America

THE GHOSTLY TALES OF VIRGINIA'S BLUE RIDGE HIGHLANDS

JOE TENNIS

Adapted from *Haunts of Virginia's Blue Ridge Highlands* by Joe Tennis

arcadia
CHILDREN'S BOOKS

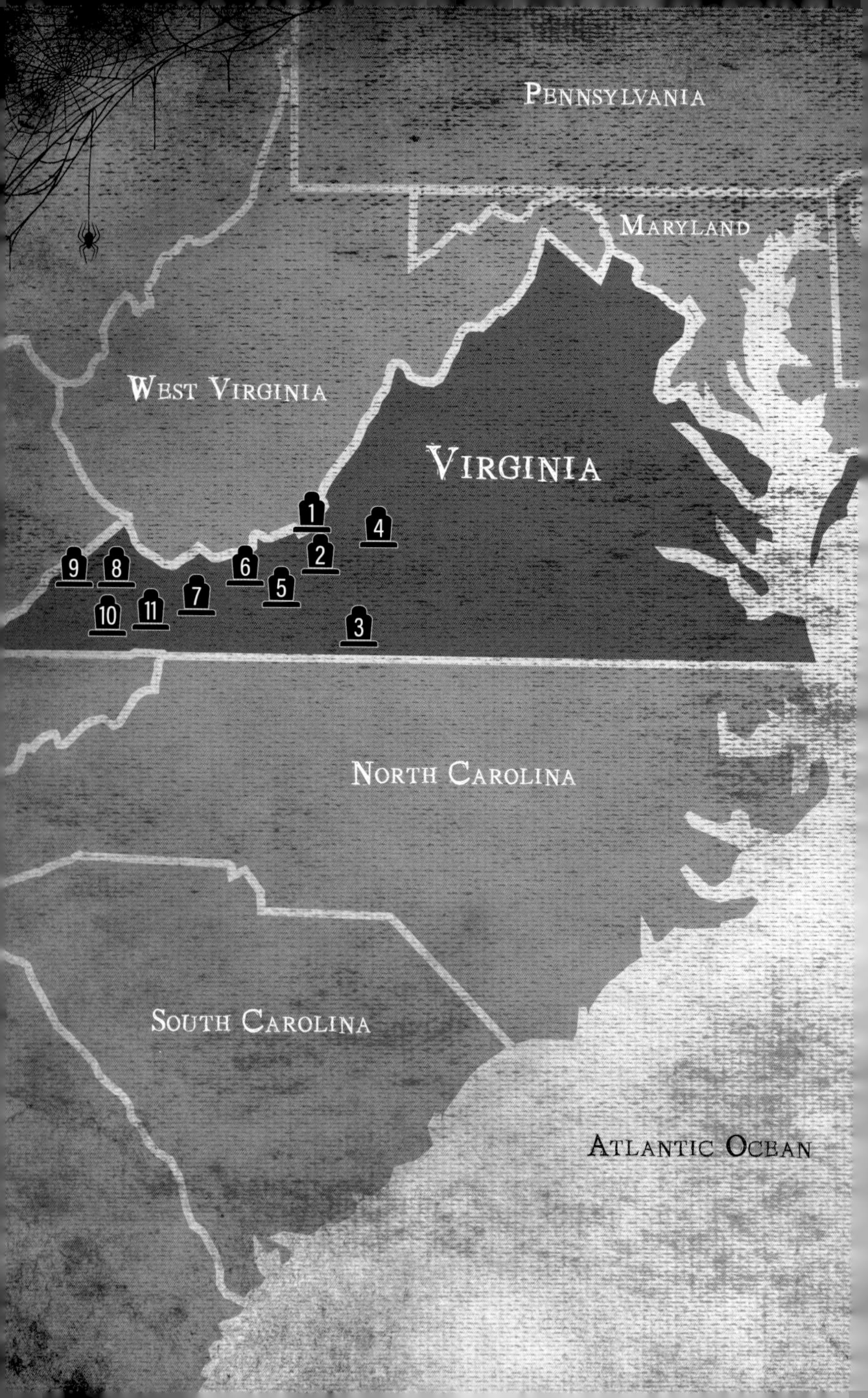

Pennsylvania
Maryland
West Virginia
Virginia
North Carolina
South Carolina
Atlantic Ocean
1
2
3
4
5
6
7
8
9
10
11

Table of Contents & Map Key

Introduction

Virginia's Blue Ridge Highlands fan across the southwest corner of the Old Dominion. The region spans both sides of the Blue Ridge, a mountain range that is topped with the famous Blue Ridge Parkway.

This area includes towns called Abingdon, Meadows of Dan, Floyd, Wytheville, Hillsville, and Independence. It was one of the last parts of Virginia to be settled. Some sections were still a wilderness as late as the 1800s—more than two centuries after the founding of the Jamestown colony in 1607.

This is a land of legends for sure. One place in Dickenson County was named Ghost Rocks by the superstitious locals who live close to this place. There's an outcropping in Wise County called Killing Rock because it was the hiding place for "the Red Fox," a man who murdered a passerby on a road leading to Kentucky in 1892. Where Norton joins Wise County in the wild woods of High Knob and Flag Rock, tales are told of the Woodbooger. It's not a ghost but a Bigfoot, believed to inhabit these deep, dark woods with elevations reaching about four thousand feet.

In Bristol, you can get started on the Mendota Trail, following the path of an old railroad. But beware if you follow that trail long enough, because you could encounter a ghost along the North Fork of the Holston River.

From Bristol to Mountain Lake, Virginia's Blue Ridge Highlands is a place full of history. So it's not surprising there are so many ghostly

stories connected to this region. In this book, you'll visit a haunted theater in Roanoke and stop at the terrifying terrain of the Major Graham Mansion, where you can see if you can bounce a ball with ghostly Clara.

See if you can spot the ghostly waiter at the Bolling Wilson Hotel or listen for the laughing boy of the Inn at Wise. Stop at the Martha Washington Inn in Abingdon. But keep your eyes open and your ears alert. Outside, you may see a ghostly horse galloping by. You may also hear the spooky strains of an unseen violin. If

so, you've just met Beth, a spirit who haunts this historic hotel.

The Ghostly Tales of Virginia's Blue Ridge Highlands shares stories of historic landmarks, a school, and a cemetery. Each chapter is based on a blend of first-hand accounts, legends, historical research, and interviews.

Mysterious Mary at Mountain Lake

The waters of Mountain Lake move on their own mysterious tide. This natural lake—one of only two natural freshwater lakes in Virginia—sits at an ear-popping elevation of 3,875 feet above sea level in Giles County. It is a unique lake in that it is kind of like a bathtub with a drain. The tub gets refilled with rain and the flow of springs. Evaporation takes away water.

Earthquakes shake the lake, causing water to seep into underground crevices.

In 1987, the lake was at full pool when its shiny waters starred in the love story of *Dirty Dancing*, a movie set in 1963. This film became a huge hit, and generations have since come to see the real-life setting of the fictional Kellerman's Mountain House from the movie, snapping shots of sites seen on screen: the hotel at Mountain Lake, the gazebo, the beach, and the Virginia Cottage.

That historic hotel, renamed Mountain Lake Lodge in 2013, was built in 1936 by William Lewis Moody. Naturally, it became a home away from home for Moody's daughter, Mary Moody Northen, who eventually became the owner.

This classy lady died at the age of ninety-four, about one month before the filming of *Dirty Dancing* began in 1986. Still, some say she has yet to leave the mountain. It's believed her ghost has shown up across the campus of what was long called the Mountain Lake Hotel.

Once, a waitress said she caught a brief glimpse of Northen's face in the wall-tall windows of the hotel dining room. The image, she said, disappeared in a couple of seconds.

Another time, hotel employee Eric Wolf said he inexplicably saw a woman staring at him from a window of the Newport Lodge, a cottage at the far end of the lake. Wolf tried to determine what could have otherwise caused this face to appear—well, other than the fact that it was a ghost. He got inside the cottage and moved furniture around and adjusted the lighting. Nothing worked to produce the face he saw.

And then? Wolf saw that woman's face staring at him again—about a year later!

When she lived here, Northen enjoyed horseback riding and relaxing along the lake's shoreline. But today, some staff members believe the ghost of mysterious Mary of Mountain Lake watches the hotel through the eyes of her own portrait. This is a carefully crafted photograph, blown up to life-size proportions, showing off all her wrinkles and rings. The picture is so large—so life-like—that it simply looks alive.

For years, this picture hung above the fireplace in the library, until 2013, when that space became a tavern. The framed photo moved to the lobby, where it hangs next to the fireplace. The photo seems normal, like something you'd see in any home. "It looks like Grandma's picture is hanging on the wall," said Jeremiah McKendree, the director of recreation and retail at Mountain Lake Lodge. Oh, but this picture is more than just a photograph.

"I've heard people say the eyes follow them as they walk through the lobby," McKendree said.

For years, too, staff members have shied away from staring too long at that picture, calling it intimidating.

Northen's eyes do appear to follow your every movement. "It looks like she's watching you, keeping an eye on you, making sure you're not bothering her things," said hotel chef Michael Porterfield.

It is also believed Northen's spirit hovers in Room 100, where she regularly stayed. This room was her summer home—and a place where little, if anything, has been altered since her death. "I think she's upset when we change things," said Porterfield, "which may be why her room has never been changed."

Possibly, her spirit in this room is restless or

even playful. Once, according to McKendree, a hotel maintenance man stayed in this room but complained that the covers would be pulled off the bed at night. It bothered him so much that he slept on the couch.

One time, his father offered to stay with him—just to see whether that was true or not. In the middle of the night, the covers were mysteriously pulled off the father, too!

For much of Northen's time, Mountain Lake remained at full pool, just as it was seen in *Dirty Dancing*. But the lake has holes where water escapes through cracks.

In 2008, the lake practically disappeared, going from its full pool of 55 acres to only 225 square feet—roughly the size of a large living room. Basically, like a bathtub, the water kept circling the drain until all that was left was a murky mess at the clogged bottom of the tub.

What was in that clog?

Well, by then, you could walk the shore and see the skeletal frames of sunken boats. Hotel guests also made an eerie discovery in the caked mud of the lake's floor: the shoes, coins, belt buckle, class ring, and bones belonging to the late Samuel Ira Felder.

This man, at the age of thirty-seven, fell off a rowboat on July 23, 1921. He was last seen choking and struggling until his body disappeared in the lake's moonlit waves. Felder's drowning happened before Northen's father built the present Mountain Lake Hotel. Several people—including a deep-sea diver

from Norfolk, Virginia—searched for Felder for the rest of the hotel season that summer. But his body was never found.

Felder's story was lost to time, unknown to the modern hotel staff until 2008. But it seems it was known to a ghostly spirit that appeared to a woman staying in a cottage during the 1990s. The woman said the ghost spoke of her son—who had drowned in the lake one night.

The Black Sisters
of Christiansburg

In the heart of Christiansburg, there is an old and spooky-looking brick school with steps labeled MONTGOMERY HALL. Built in the 1930s, it was once home to Blacksburg Middle School and Christiansburg High School. This site has connections to the century-old tale of the Black Sisters.

The Montgomery Female Academy once stood on this same site in the early 1900s before this school was built. That academy was a boarding school where girls would live while studying. Three old sisters—Virginia Wardlaw, Mary Snead, and Caroline Martin—ran the school until it closed in 1908.

These sisters all wore large black hats and black robes, shrouding their faces with long, black veils. To the good Christians of Christiansburg, such funeral-style fashions earned them the nickname "the Black Sisters."

The town talked a lot about the Black Sisters. They just didn't behave the way everyone else did. And then they were embroiled in a scandal. They pressured Mary's son, John Snead, to leave his wife in Tennessee and help run the school. So he came. But misfortune followed him everywhere.

John nearly got killed falling off a train in Roanoke. Then he fell into a cistern at their school in Christiansburg. (A cistern is a large tank often used to hold water.) He recovered from that, but was then found screaming in a burning bed! It had been soaked with kerosene and set on fire. He died within hours from severe burns. Local police suspected foul play, and so did the attending physician. Suspicion fell on the Black Sisters. But why would they harm one of their own children? Was everything that happened to John Snead an accident? Or were the sisters involved?

Either by need or by greed, the sisters dodged arrest and successfully made a claim on an insurance policy taken on John's life. In other words, they collected money because he died. Obviously, John's death was suspicious. And so were the sisters' strange habits. Oh, how the town talked.

By night, these sisters would creep off with a wagon driver who would take them to a cemetery in Christiansburg. There, the driver would later say, these women would perform rituals at a particular grave.

Back on campus at the Montgomery Female Academy, the Black Sisters installed excessive locks on doors. They seemed to be paranoid. They moved students from room to room, seemingly for no reason. The Black Sisters would also sometimes be found standing over the young girls as they slept in the dormitory.

With all this oddity, practically the entire town of Christiansburg grew afraid of these witchy women. Their school grew less and less popular. It racked up debt, and the sisters fled town in 1909. A few months later,

Christiansburg townsfolk heard the news that Caroline Martin's beautiful young daughter Ocey had drowned in a bathtub in East Orange, New Jersey.

Much like John Snead's death in the burning bed at Christiansburg, Ocey's death looked suspicious. Once again, the sisters tried to get money and make an insurance claim. Only this time, police intervened, and the sisters met their own frightening fate.

Caroline pleaded guilty to murdering her daughter and was sent to prison; Mary was tried as an accomplice and released to the custody of her son Albert. Virginia Wardlaw, the unmarried sister, somehow never went to trial. This woman in black simply starved herself to death before the trial began.

Back in Christiansburg, the legend of the Black Sisters lives on. Generations of students have sworn of the spookiness of the school site, built on the same site as the now-gone Black Sisters' school. Often, they said, they could hear the sounds of high-heeled shoes walking through the hallways. The Black Sisters never actually entered *this* building, but their restless spirits may have settled here after their old school was torn down.

Christiansburg mayor Richard Ballengee worked here as a teacher and principal for more than twenty-five years. In the 1960s, he recalled hearing high heels "clop-clop-clop-clop" across a wooden floor when no one was around.

School custodian Sue Robinette said she heard what sounded like high heels walking down the hall, too. "And I looked, and there was nobody there," she said.

Whose shoes made these mysterious footstep sounds? Could that have been the ghosts of the Black Sisters? Who knows?

With a smile, Ballengee said, "I kind of took pride as principal. I would go to Richmond and say, 'You know, I'm the only principal in Virginia with a haunted school.'"

Fright Nights at the Reynolds Homestead

It was a hot, humid, and very starless night when I followed the long, dark driveway to reach the remote Reynolds Homestead in the Blue Ridge Highlands of Patrick County.

I arrived alone on this steamy Saturday in June. And, yes, it was still hot at 11:00 p.m. But in addition to the weather, I felt a particularly odd sense of heat on the back of my neck, like an electrical sensation, as I stood at the back door of the brick Reynolds Homestead.

The Reynolds Homestead has stood near a crossroads called Critz since 1843. Most famously, this was the birthplace of Richard Joshua "R.J." Reynolds, a tobacco businessman whose company created Camel cigarettes.

Coming here, I knew some of the Reynolds family history. I knew R.J. had a little brother named Hardin Harbour Reynolds. Harbour owned a tobacco factory that went up in flames at South Boston. His young daughter also died on Christmas Day in 1912 because of a fire.

I also knew that people had not only been born but had also died inside this house. Such stories would serve as the focus of my talk at the visitor center on that following Sunday.

I had seen this house once, on a sunny day, while conducting research on the Reynolds family. But I had never been to the upstairs apartment, which the staff offered to me as a place to stay.

As I turned the key at the back door this night, I felt short of breath and uneasy.

Yes, I had been invited. But I felt like I was intruding into someone's home. Still, I needed a place to stay. This plantation was three hours from home.

With sweaty palms, I entered the museum exhibit space downstairs. I flipped on a light and stayed reverently quiet, as if I didn't want to wake anyone, even though I was alone.

Slowly, I reached the top of the stairs. I stared with wide-eyed wonder at every detail on every wall as my mind suddenly slowed to a crawl. Just beyond a small room known as the library, I slipped through the bedroom to find the bathroom. There, I was startled when I saw a mouse dart across the floor.

But I felt flat-out frightened when I walked through a cold spot in the bedroom, just

outside the bathroom door. It was like passing through an invisible refrigerator about one foot wide. Was that cold spot a place where a ghost was standing?

I did not want to find out. I simply hurried away, running from the bedroom to the library and across the hall. There, I locked myself inside the semimodern kitchen. And there I felt safe, but only as safe as somebody who was about six years old, not forty.

I stood in the kitchen and tried to catch my breath. But my mind was now racing. So was my heartbeat. There was something, I was convinced, something beyond that kitchen door—some presence. And that presence did not want me here with it.

Finding a phone on the kitchen counter, I called my wife in a panic. "Do you see anything?" she asked me.

"No," I said.

"Do you hear anything?" she asked me.

"No," I said.

"Do you smell anything?" she asked me.

"No," I said. "But I know there's something in here. And it does not want me here with it."

"Well then," she said, "you'd best get out of there!"

And so I did. I unlocked the door and scurried down the stairs. In a flash, I hit the highway for a half-hour, going east to Martinsville.

Briefly, I contemplated sleeping in my car. Then, more sensibly, I searched for a new place to stay. But, by now, it was close to 1:00 a.m., and it seemed like every motel had already closed.

I did finally find a motel that was still open and accepting guests. But the clerk wanted nearly one hundred dollars for what I figured would be a less-than-desirable room. So I left.

Then, bravely, I retreated to the Reynolds Homestead to face my fears. Back again at the backyard of the big brick house, I bypassed the gnarly and twisted limbs of the creepy catalpa tree that looked like it wanted to grab something—or somebody—on the lawn.

Then, like a small child afraid of his grandmother's ghost, I rushed back up the stairs to that semimodern kitchen and locked the door. Again, I felt safe but still scared. I turned on all the lights. And I cranked up rock music on the radio as I fell asleep on the couch at 2:00 a.m.

The next morning, the sun shone. And, surprisingly, I had not a single fear, but I really did not have the guts to go downstairs.

Around noon, the kitchen telephone rang. It was Beth Almond Ford, a longtime historical services assistant at the Reynolds Homestead. She asked me how I had slept. And I told her, embarrassingly enough, just how freaked out I got.

"Oh, Joe," Ford said with calm tone, "we have guests tell us all the time that they have experiences here. I have always felt a presence in the house, each and every time I go into it. It's never been frightening nor the least bit scary, but it is as if there are spirits present."

Once, Ford said, a woman from South America felt a presence in the home and even stated that she saw several male apparitions over the course of two nights. Another time, an artist-in-residence staying here in the 1990s felt especially troubled, Ford said.

"As she was sleeping the first night, she woke up to find an elderly 'man' grabbing onto her arm and refusing to let go," Ford said. "The next day, she walked around the house, the graveyards and the grounds. Ford said that the artist told the spirits—whoever they were— that all must coexist peacefully, and she really needed to get her sleep.

Perhaps my fear came from what I already knew—specifically, what had happened to all the children. In 1862, an inoculation gone wrong turned into a tragedy. Hardin Reynolds, the father of R.J. and Harbour, hastily vaccinated his children for smallpox—at a risk. At that time, vaccinations were not always considered safe. And, in less than a week, three of the Reynolds children died—two boys and a girl, all under the age of seven, all suffering the aftereffects of the vaccine.

I also kept thinking about little Nancy Ruth Reynolds, Harbour's six-year-old daughter who died fifty years later in a Christmas calamity.

On that Sunday afternoon, I delivered my speech. It was well received. But the audience seemed most intrigued when I mentioned my fright night at the Reynolds Homestead. Like me, they wanted to figure out who was haunting this house.

The homestead director, in turn, told me that day that she had a similar experience when she spent a restless night here. Like me, she had the feeling of being glued wide-open to every one of her senses and not knowing why.

In later months, I would meet Sharon Kroeller, a longtime Reynolds Homestead volunteer who shared that she, too, had

sensed something. "I could feel the presence of people," she said. "When I feel a presence, I have a very heavy feeling on my chest. I have heart palpitations. And there's almost a feeling of adrenaline that runs through me." It was the same thing that I sensed.

Downstairs in the living room, Kroeller felt a particular heavy presence next to the fireplace—a sense that there had been a catastrophe. In the second-floor library, where I had turned so lifeless, she felt more: "I smelled smoke—not pipe smoke, not cigar smoke. I felt heaviness throughout the upstairs. But the room that I got focused on, for whatever reason, was that room with the smell—the smoke smell." It was the library that also had me frozen cold like a child, snagged by every detail of every book.

It was in the library as well that Kroeller had sensed many men rushing around in frenzy.

"And I sensed men, as opposed to women or children," she said. "I just felt the heaviness up there, that there was a presence and there was hustle and bustle in there, that there was a lot going on in that room."

In this same vicinity, Reynolds Homestead administrative assistant Terrill Levine once reported hearing giggling children at the top of the stairs. And, she said, this happened when there was no one else in the house.

In the daylight after my fright night, I followed the precedent of that guest artist who had stayed in the upstairs apartment: I went outside and walked the graveyard.

There, I focused on little Nancy Ruth Reynolds. It was her story that I had already known and one that had both touched and troubled me. In 1912, she reached for her Christmas stocking on a fireplace mantel. But her nightgown caught fire, and she died after deeply inhaling the smoke. But where did that happen? Was it in the library, where Sharon Kroeller had smelled smoke? Was there a "catastrophe" at the Reynolds Homestead fireplace? Or did this happen someplace else?

For years, it was told, little Nancy died at the Reynolds Homestead. Her body is buried in the family cemetery—just a few yards from the house. But let's play detective, because that story does not match what was printed in a newspaper nearly six weeks after Nancy's death.

"She begged her parents to allow her to go to Danville with her teacher to spend a few days at Christmas," says the obituary, published in the February 13, 1913, edition of the *Enterprise* at Stuart. "At first, they tried to dissuade her and her father seemed to have a foreboding of danger."

Still, Harbour and his wife, Annie, made all necessary preparations—and, according to the newspaper, the six-year-old girl traveled by train to spend the holiday away from her parents at Danville. There, the obituary says, Nancy met her final fate: "On Christmas morning, as she was standing in front of an open grate looking at her presents her clothing caught fire and she was fatally injured. In ten minutes she was in bed in a Danville hospital with three physicians and a trained nurse in attendance." The newspaper says, "At four o'clock in the afternoon, she fell into a peaceful sleep to wake in that 'better land.'"

Is this true? Is that story fact or fiction? Did Nancy really spend the Christmas holiday away from her parents when she was only six years old? And is the haunting of the Reynolds Homestead connected to Nancy's tragedy?

Consider this evidence: Beth Almond Ford says she once had a home tour interrupted by a first-time female visitor. Suddenly, Ford said, this woman was startled by the ghostly vision of a little girl with her clothes in flames in the downstairs living room. What do you think? Did she die in Danville or in her own home?

Today, a marble lamb sits atop Nancy's gravestone as she sleeps forever in that better land.

Before leaving on that Sunday after my lecture, I thanked that little girl for letting me stay a night in her house. And, with a prayer, I told her I was sorry that she had died so young.

Ghostly Grandin Theatre of Roanoke

Roanoke's stately Grandin Theatre first opened its doors in 1932, during the difficult days of the Great Depression. It remained a movie house for more than forty years until going dark in 1976, only to later reopen.

Through the years, employees such as Cat Conover began sharing stories of spooky spaces and haunted happenings at the Grandin, where the main auditorium seats more than 300.

It's believed that a film projectionist suffered a heart attack here, which might explain some of the Grandin's ghostly stuff. "I actually had something stroke my leg once, up in the projectionist booth," said Conover, a projections manager.

One longstanding story says that during one of the many times the Grandin Theatre was closed, it was once home to a family experiencing homelessness. Assistant manager Sean Poff said that two of the family's children died here. And now, it's said that you can sometimes hear a baby crying in the theater's spooky stairwell. "There are a lot of strange sounds in here," Conover said. "The theater, itself, has a spirit. You can feel the theater. We love the spirits here."

Perhaps the most spine-tingling spirit of the Grandin Theatre belongs to a mysterious boy. Could he possibly be related to the family's lost children? As this story goes, a projectionist reportedly saw a young boy on the stairs late one night, long after all screens went dark and the movies had ended. This projectionist said he figured the boy was lost or had even been left behind. So at first, he followed the boy, step by step. They went up the stairs.

And then? Well, as the story is told, that boy just vanished when he walked into a door! What do you think? Is there a ghost boy in this theater who sees all the shows for free? Maybe he loves the movies so much he never wants to leave.

CHAPTER 5

Music at the Major Graham Mansion

Outside Grahams Forge, there's a historic landmark on a hillside that looks like the haunted house of anyone's nightmare. It's a two-faced place with a strong and straight brick front on one side and Victorian double porches with curves like mournful half-moons on another. A cone-shaped top on the roof looks like a witch's hat.

This imposing brick fortress took its name from Major David Graham, a Confederate army officer. The Graham family amassed a fortune building iron furnaces that roared all over Wythe County. In the 1800s, members of the Graham family fought in the Civil War.

In the late 1900s, decades after the Grahams no longer owned this estate, people reported seeing shadows around the property. They also saw mysterious faces in the windows of the remote mansion, tucked away along snake-shaped roads near Cedar Run.

By 2010, folks also talked about Clara, a little girl ghost who was believed to have been an orphan cared for by the Graham family. No one knows if there really was a Clara, much less what she looked like. But team after team of ghost investigators have come here, seeking to speak with who they believe is Clara.

It also seems that a ghost with musical connections could inhabit the Major Graham mansion. Country music singer J.C. Weaver bought the Graham property in 1988, but he did not live in the mansion. It remained vacant. Weaver would entertain friends in the empty mansion by singing songs and playing guitar and piano, much like his musical heroes, the Southern rock band Lynyrd Skynyrd. In 2007, Weaver launched Grahamfest, a music festival that featured a performance by Weaver as well as the Roanoke Symphony Orchestra on a large stage not far from the mansion.

For the 2009 festival, Weaver hired a Lynyrd Skynyrd tribute band called Long Island Street Survivors. (This band took its name from "Street Survivors," the haunting final record released by the original Lynyrd Skynyrd just three days before their plane crashed and killed the band's original singer in 1977). Joining the Long Island Street Survivors on stage were two members of the original Lynyrd Skynyrd. On a microphone was backup singer JoJo Billingsley, who was temporarily out of the band in 1977

but did have a horrifying nightmare that the band's plane was going to crash just hours before it did.

On drums was the long-haired Artimus Pyle—the only Lynyrd Skynyrd band member physically able to climb out of the plane crash wreckage and go for help. "I can't believe this place that we're playing tonight," Pyle said onstage. "I've played all over the world, and this is an unusual, incredible place with a great history." Both Billingsley and Pyle walked the

grounds outside the Major Graham Mansion on that Saturday. But despite the audience's enthusiasm for songs like "What's Your Name" and Weaver helping sing "Free Bird," these rock stars would never play this place again. Grahamfest ended after that. Sadly, Billingsley died from cancer less than a year later.

As for the Major Graham Mansion, it took a tantalizing turn toward a spooky world. It opened to the public as an annual haunted house, blaring loud music, including Lynyrd Skynyrd songs. There were plenty of props, such as skulls, spiders, and snakes. Inside the mansion, kids loved to visit "Clara's Room," where they tried to test the spirit of the orphan girl, seeing if Clara would roll a ball back to them across the floor. But let's not forget that this mansion is also *really* haunted.

Ghost hunters who have visited here have recorded strange messages including one that said "I don't play that tune," spoken by a voice believed to be a ghost. Another time, an unexplained voice asked, "What's your name?"

Now, that could have been a question or it could have been a request. Perhaps whatever haunts the mansion is a Lynyrd Skynyrd fan. Maybe Grahamfest stirred up the spirits. And now it wants to hear that band's famous song "What's Your Name" one more time.

But wait—there is still more music at Major Graham Mansion. "The spirits that live in this house are unbelievable," Weaver said in 2019. "I used to play the piano, and there would be spirits that would hum with me."

CHAPTER 6

Bolling Wilson Hotel of Wytheville

Donald Daugherty worked at the front desk of George Wythe Hotel in downtown Wytheville during the mid-1960s. He is "a skeptic" when it comes to ghosts. But, he said, "There's a specific event that I can't explain."

At the wee hour of 2 a.m. on a Sunday night, Daugherty thought he was alone at the front desk. Then the door to the basement opened, and a well-dressed elderly man wearing a winter coat walked into the lobby.

This man carried an umbrella. He put a glove on his left hand then another glove on his right. He placed a round-top hat on his head. Then, according to Daugherty, he tipped that hat and walked out the side door.

"It was strange," Daugherty said. "And I thought, 'Who was that at 2 o'clock in the morning?'"

Daugherty told a hotel bellhop named James Kelley what he had seen, but that bellhop, according to Daugherty, did not act surprised.

"He was a waiter here," the bellhop said. "And he died."

"Died?" Daugherty wondered. So, wait, if this waiter was now dead, well, that must mean that Daugherty had seen . . . a ghost!

And, if so, perhaps the presence of a ghostly waiter could also explain why Daugherty would sometimes hear a mysterious tinkling noise coming from the direction of the dining room even though it was empty at the time. That, according to Daugherty, was the unexplained clanging of plates and spoons, like somebody— or some ghost—was resetting the tables for an event. "I always heard the dining room tinkling," Daugherty said. Perhaps, too, that ghostly waiter still wanders the building—now called the Bolling Wilson Hotel.

Tess Monday, a front desk clerk in 2019, said she saw a mysterious man in the hotel gift shop. He was wearing a black coat and a tall, rounded hat, she said. "And when I went to say 'hi' to him, it's just like he vanished into thin air. It gave me goosebumps."

Bolling Wilson Hotel takes its name from Edith Bolling Wilson, the second wife of President Woodrow Wilson. He served in the White House during World War I. Edith was born just across Main Street from the hotel, in a second-floor apartment on October 12, 1872.

The George Wythe Hotel was built in 1927. It closed in 1973 and reopened as the Bolling Wilson Hotel in 2014 with plush and elegant furnishings. In between its different periods as a hotel, this brick building became a bank. For a while, the structure also housed tenants in apartments—including one woman who "looked like she combed her hair with a vacuum cleaner," said Gilbert "Tinker" Jones, a longtime maintenance man at the bank during the 1980s and 1990s.

For sure, that woman's multicolored hair seemed scary. But what really jolted Jones was seeing "a man standing in the bookkeeping department that come through a door that there was only one key to it. And I had it on my keyring," Jones said.

The mystery man wore gray work clothes on this day in the 1980s, Jones said. "He was just a normal individual. There wasn't anything extraordinary about him—just a common person," Jones said. "He stood there a minute. He looked down the hall at me. He turned around, come to the front of the building." Then the man disappeared, Jones said. "Where he went, I don't know. I looked."

Several former bank employees like Jones reported haunted happenings—from hearing phantom footsteps to witnessing the elevator presumably operated by invisible passengers.

One night, bank employee Donna Gillespie heard the elevator door opening on the second floor. Next, she heard a knock on the stairwell door. Gillespie ignored that knock a couple of times. "Then I jerked the door open," she said. "And there wasn't anybody there."

On late nights in the 1980s, bank employee Kathy Smith worked in the bank's collections department, often staying to 10:00 p.m., when no one else was in the building. Yet that's when she noticed the elevator door would open to the third floor. "And there was nobody there," she said. "And then, all of a sudden, you heard every toilet on the floor flush at once."

Often, bank employees said, the toilets in this building would flush on their own. As a maintenance man, Gilbert Jones would run to check the toilet-flushing sound. But he said that no evidence of flushing water could be found. It was just noisy commodes. Toilet paper would also vanish from a particular closet, bank employees said.

"The things that I remember are the things that went missing," said longtime bank employee Benita Jones. "Toilet paper would disappear. But we never saw anybody. If somebody was carrying something out, we would have seen them." In time, the people at the bank began believing that the building's ghosts also took more than toilet paper. Benita Jones said you could lay an item on your desk, and it would disappear. "Then, the next morning, there it would be."

Once, too, on a day in the 1990s, bank employee Kathy Smith said her typewriter seemingly began typing all by itself. "It was just different letters," she said. "It was wild!" After a while, bank employees came up with names for the alleged ghosts, "Trish" and

"Josh," and they blamed this pair for whatever mischief occurred.

On the third floor, Donna Gillespie tried to warn a couple of visitors one afternoon to watch out for the bank's stuff-swiping ghosts. "Y'all be careful," she said to a couple of computer repairmen. "We've got ghosts in this area. Their names are Trish and Josh."

One man heard the warning but still said they were going to leave their tools for the night. To that, Gillespie said, "Don't be surprised if it's not there when you come in."

Well, you might have guessed—that's what happened. The next morning, that same man stood with wide-eyed wonder. He looked at the tables and cried, "Our stuff is gone!"

"Look on the fourth floor," Gillespie suggested. "Trish and Josh must have decided they needed it." Sure enough, that's where all was found.

CHAPTER 7

Haunts of the Herb House

The Herb House, at 107 Pendleton Street (just off Marion's Main Street), was built in 1916. The brick structure became known as the "Herb House" because R.T. Greer and Company used herbs, berries, and roots to make medicine at this location until 1968. The building stood vacant for decades, until it was restored in the 1990s as a craft shop. It later became an art store and ice cream parlor where a ghostly girl has been heard and possibly seen.

Holly Thomas spent a couple of years inside the Herb House producing art, serving ice cream, and studying the spirits. "You could be walking in that building, and it felt like somebody was playing with the back of your neck or your hair," Thomas said.

Thomas and her husband, Jim, would report feeling mysterious tugs on their legs inside the building. Jim Thomas also heard a little girl's voice—and a laugh—when there was clearly no little girl in the building.

After that, Holly Thomas enlisted the help of Marion Virginia Paranormal Investigations, a ghost investigation group. This team used voice recorders and cameras all over the three-story building. While the group members were researching, a rock was thrown at them by an unseen presence.

But that's not all. Holly Thomas reported hearing the ghostly girl laughing or playing one night around 9:00 p.m. in the ice cream parlor. "And there was no one there," Thomas said.

"I can't deny that I heard that voice. And I can't deny the fact that I heard a child laughing," she said. "It sounded like a little girl about maybe four years old."

According to legend, Thomas said, a young girl with some connection to the Greer family (who operated the Herb House) died during the mid-1900s. Now, possibly, she said, that's why this girl's spirit shows herself with pranks such as turning on the tap water in a sink when no one else is around.

In addition to art and ice cream, Thomas sold dolls at the Herb House. One morning, she came in to find one particular doll out of the display case and standing up on the

floor, as if a little girl had pulled it down and wanted to play.

On another night in 2014, around 9:00 pm, Thomas saw a shadow. "It was moving fast," she said. "It went across the floor. It was like the shadow of a dog. It was scary.

It was unnatural. It wasn't moving like a creature or an animal. It was smaller, like a child would be, standing up."

Could it be that the little girl ghost of the Herb House was up past her bedtime?

Castlewood Cemetery

It's believed that lost Civil War graves lie beneath the lawn of Bick and Judy Gibson's Russell County home. It's located in a quiet community called Mud Hole Store near Castlewood, on the outskirts of St. Paul. The house was built for Dr. Samuel Wesley Gibson and his wife, Harriet, during the war in 1863.

As many as eight hundred Southern soldiers once camped here after crossing the nearby Clinch River during the Civil War. This camp was called "Many Sinks" for the many sinkholes in the ground.

Connecting clues, historians from Kentucky pinpointed the lawn outside the Gibsons' stately home as the location of seemingly endless rows of Confederate graves. They used dowsing rods to determine the location of the graves.

"They say there's all kinds of people buried here, all over the top of this mountain," Bick Gibson said. "All across the top of this knob are graves."

The graves weren't just from the war. This was also a local cemetery for the Castlewood community and, possibly, a repository for the many arms and legs amputated by Dr. Gibson at his doctor's office during the Civil War. There might be big pile of body parts under the lawn, Gibson said.

As late as the 1930s, stones marked the graves. But as those original stones fell over, they were taken down and stacked in a barn. Then they disappeared, lending even more mystery to the Castlewood cemetery. Nobody seems to know where the stones are today.

Perhaps, with all this loss, it's no surprise that ghosts have been seen in this area.

One man contacted the Gibsons to say that his twelve-year-old daughter would describe spooky visions to her parents whenever she passed the house. This girl witnessed the ghostly figures of soldiers dressed in gray uniforms wandering between the house and the cemetery.

This girl could also see Dr. Gibson, with white hair and a white beard, sitting in a rocking chair on a porch as his wife served him tea. Quite eerily, the porch that girl described is no longer there!

Another time, a man from Louisiana visited the cemetery to see a few graves that now do have modern markers noting the burial of dead soldiers.

"You know, we're not alone," the man said to Bick Gibson.

"Do you see a deer or something on the creek?" Gibson asked.

"No," the stranger returned. "There's a ghost of a soldier on the creek, watching. There

are two spirits or something on that hillside—a lost soldier's spirit, and he has not found his way."

Who knows how many other soldiers' spirits wander this area of Virginia?

Laughing Boy of the Inn at Wise

One night, around 9:00, a group of boys took off running in the second-floor hallways of the Inn at Wise. These middle-schoolers had come here from Northern Virginia to compete in an athletic competition at the nearby University of Virginia's College at Wise.

Suddenly, one of the boys tripped and fell on what seemed like absolutely nothing! At least, the boy would say, there was nothing in the way. As he lifted himself off the floor, however, the boy heard something in his ear— the laughter of a little boy. But there was no little boy in sight!

Freaked out, the running boys ran down to the front desk of the century-old hotel.

"Are there ghosts here?" the boys asked in a panic.

"Of course," said the assistant manager, Corey Dotson.

The staff of the Inn at Wise have identified four ghosts along the hallways and forty-nine rooms of the historic hotel, which is painted white and fronted by columns and porches.

Among the spirits are a little boy and a little girl. They are unseen—and their origins unknown—yet they are believed to play pranks or jump on beds that have just been made by the housekeeping staff, Dotson said. "The only reason they know it's a boy and girl is the giggles and the laughs that they hear."

Once known as the Colonial Hotel, the Inn at Wise was built in 1910, at the height of Wise County's coal boom along the Kentucky-Virginia border. The classy Colonial Hotel attracted businessmen as well as families who wanted to enjoy the mountains and slumber in style during the mid-1900s. But eventually the Colonial closed. For a while in the 1970s, the hotel became an apartment house. Later, the structure stood vacant and decaying next to the Wise County Courthouse. But in 2014, the hotel reopened, restored and refreshed. Each room in the restored section has a unique shape. The luxurious lobby includes tulip-shaped iron chandeliers.

On the second floor, it's said you can see "the Pink Nightgown Lady," the spirit of a wispy woman who appears to float through the

hallway late at night. No facial features have been reported, but you can see her long hair, Dotson said.

And then there's "Henry." This ghost showed up in the Colonial Dining Room, standing against a column one morning at 11:00 in March 2021.

On that day, three hotel staff members tested a heat sensor app on a cell phone, and the sensor captured the image of a person—possibly a man—leaning against the column at the center of the room. That ghostly image had one leg up and a foot propped against the column, said Megan Scicli, a front desk manager.

"It scared me to death. I saw it with my own two eyes. It freaked me out," she said. "It even showed the points of the body. It showed the actual lines."

The staff believes Henry was a writer who was staying as a guest at the old Dotson Hotel, which burned down on this site prior to 1910. Folks figure Henry lost his life in that fire.

Now, in Room 337, lights flash and things move, according to Dotson. "Room 337 is actually dedicated as 'Henry's Room,' " Dotson said.

Employees also reportedly see a hunched-over black figure in the hotel, Dotson said.

"And you can tell it's an older man," Dotson said. "Henry is typically thought of as the quiet one. But if you hear odd noises or things moving, that's usually Henry."

Perhaps Henry paid a visit to a room on the second floor in 2018. There, according to Dotson, a corporate official said he saw a black figure appear in his room's doorway for a solid forty-five seconds. This man talked to the figure. He said hello. But there was no reply.

Checking out the room's lighting, the man went to the window and tried to see if he could move the shade and produce the same shadow.

He couldn't. And about that same time, the figure disappeared.

The man went to sleep. The next morning, the man walked into the shower and found a mysterious puddle in what had been a clean and spotless bathroom. Where that came

from, according to Dotson, no one could ever explain. Did Henry take a quick shower? We may never know.

Ghost of the Mendota Trail

Like the nearby and more famous Virginia Creeper Trail, the Mendota Trail follows the path of an old railroad line. Both rail trails once connected to the main line of tracks that rolls down the valley from Roanoke to Christiansburg, Wytheville, Marion, Abingdon, and Bristol.

The Mendota Trail links Bristol to Benhams on a five-mile path. But its original railroad line spans beyond Benhams to reach the mountains of Mendota after snaking through the wilderness of the Wolf Run Gorge.

This was once called the Bristol Coal & Iron Narrow-Gauge Railroad, later to be known as the South Atlantic & Ohio Railway. It was part of the Southern Railway when trains stopped running in 1972. The train tracks were then used for a short-lived scenic excursion train on which riders could get an up-close view of Clinch Mountain in Washington County.

Mendota (pronounced "men-DOUGH-tah") is said to be a Native American word that means "bend in the river" (the North Fork of the Holston River).

In the place where the river meets the railroad is where you may encounter the ghost of the Mendota Trail. There is a bridge here that can be reached after walking one mile from the Mendota Trailhead at the west. This bridge stands just above a tiny cave into which the river flows.

Who knows who has gone into that cave? But perhaps this was the final resting place of a prisoner who escaped from a convict work camp here in 1879, when the original railroad trestle was built. The story goes that the prisoner took a fatal fall while trying to escape life on the chain gang. It's said that his body was never recovered.

But did his spirit try to climb back on that bridge? Just after the prisoner disappeared, convicts continuing to work on the bridge said they felt their ankles being grabbed by cold hands!

After dark, it gets even scarier. That's when, some say, you can look into the river and see the prisoner's spirit show up as a strange light in the water.

CHAPTER 11

Beth's Violin at Martha Washington Inn

Well-heeled young ladies arrived in the genteel town of Abingdon as early as 1860 to attend the Martha Washington College for Women. Here, they studied English, French, piano, and math in the many-chimneyed brick campus buildings on Abingdon's Main Street.

One of the buildings was constructed in 1832 as a private mansion for General Francis

Preston and his large family. In this stately setting, those who became known as the "Martha Girls" had to abide by a variety of

rules. The young men at nearby Emory & Henry College loved to ask the Martha Girls for dates by mailing letters. But the Martha Girls were only allowed to reply if they got permission from the college president. Martha Girls also could not wave at the train conductors as they passed on the tracks behind the college.

Under such restrictions, the Martha Girls looked for escapes beyond the confines of the campus. At night, these women told ghost stories, largely centered on when the college became a temporary Civil War hospital—just a few years after the college opened.

Students of the newly opened college became nurses when their college building— now a luxury hotel called the Martha Washington Inn—served as a medical facility and refuge from the war.

In 1864, Abingdon saw wartime action when Union general George Stoneman and his troops raided the town. A lone soldier hung around later and set fire to the Washington County Courthouse. That arsonist was shot out of the saddle on his horse by Confederates. He died.

It's believed that man's ghostly horse runs around town still looking for its rider, especially in the vicinity of the Martha Washington Inn.

The Martha Girls often told the ghost story of a runaway horse that many have since claimed to see on the hotel lawn or along Main Street.

In addition to the spirited steed, the Martha  Girls whispered words about Beth. She was said to have been a student nurse during the Civil War. She was also in love with a wounded

Yankee officer, whom she tried to comfort by playing her violin. But that love faced tragedy.

The officer knew he was going to perish. So he called out, "Play something, Beth. Play something. I'm going to die!" With that, Beth played a melody on her violin as the man slipped into an eternal sleep.

Beth, too, would die, a victim of typhoid fever, it has been told. Now, it's said, you can go to the Martha Washington Inn and sometimes hear Beth's ghost playing her violin.

This often-told story made its way into brochures promoting "The Martha," as the hotel is affectionately known.

Over the years, guests and staff say they have heard music or even seen sprits inside the main hotel building. Once, a man staying on the hotel's third floor rushed down to the lobby, saying, "I've heard it. I've heard your musical ghost." The front desk clerk tried to assure the man that everything was OK. The clerk followed the man to the third floor.

Standing in the hallway, all was silent at first. But then the music played. And, yes, it was a violin playing a tune! Could it have been the ghost of Beth?

Was there really a musical ghost at the Martha? Well, maybe not on this night. As it turned out, the man who reported hearing the ghostly violin music was staying in a room next to a concert violinist who was scheduled

to play later that night at nearby Emory &
Henry College.

So, you can believe in ghostly tales—or not.

Our ghost tour through the Blue Ridge
Highlands comes to a close here. Do you
believe these ghosts are real? Or just stories
and legends? Maybe you should stop in to
some of these places and see for yourself!"

About the Author

Joe Tennis is a graduate of Radford University. He is the author of books on history and legends of Virginia, Tennessee, and North Carolina. His other books include *Haunts of Virginia's Blue Ridge Highlands*, *Virginia Rail Trails: Crossing the Commonwealth*, and *Along Virginia's Route 58: True Tales from Beach to Bluegrass*.

Joe Tennis is the author of books on history and legends of Virginia, Tennessee and North Carolina. His other books include *Haunts of Virginia's Blue Ridge Highlands*, *Virginia Rail Trails: Crossing the Commonwealth* and *Along Virginia's Route 58: True Tales from Beach to Bluegrass*.

Check out some of the other Spooky America titles available now!

Spooky America was adapted from the creeptastic Haunted America series for adults. Haunted America explores historical haunts in cities and regions across America. Each book chronicles both the widely known and less-familiar history behind local ghosts and other unexplained mysteries. Here's more from author Joe Tennis:

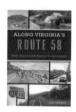